CONSERVATIVE COLORING BOOK

From Reagan to Jefferson

ARTHUR BENJAMIN

This page intentionally left blank.

ABOUT THE BOOK

Get in touch with conservative principles coloring conservative heroes from Reagan to Jefferson. Great for kids and adults alike, this book is great for anyone who stands for conservative values.

Printed in the United States of America
ISBN: 978-1619495449

CONTENTS

This page intentionally left blank.

Thomas Jefferson

Plate 1.

That government is best which governs least

James Madison

Plate 2.

John Randolph

Plate 3.

US HOUSE OF REPRESENTATIVES

Nathaniel Macon

Plate 4.

John C. Calhoun

Plate 5.

Grover Clebeland

Plate 6.

Calvin Coolidge

Plate 7.

Ronald Reagan

Plate 8.

This page intentionally left blank.

ABOUT THE BOOK

Get in touch with conservative principles coloring conservative heroes from Reagan to Jefferson. Great for kids and adults alike, this book is great for anyone who stands for conservative values.

www.ingramcontent.com/pod-product-compliance
Lightning Source LLC
Chambersburg PA
CBHW081236020426

42331CB00012B/3205